MW00398072

Clear Speech
Teacher's Manual and Answer Key

Clear Speech

Pronunciation and Listening Comprehension in American English

Teacher's Manual and Answer Key

Judy B. Gilbert

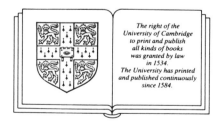

The right of the
University of Cambridge
to print and publish
all kinds of books
was granted by law
in 1534.
The University has printed
and published continuously
since 1584.

Cambridge University Press

Cambridge

New York   New Rochelle

Melbourne   Sydney

Published by the Press Syndicate of the University of Cambridge
The Pitt Building, Trumpington Street, Cambridge CB2 1RP
32 East 57th Street, New York, NY 10022, USA
10 Stamford Road, Oakleigh, Melbourne 3166, Australia

First published 1984
Fourth printing 1988

Printed in the United States of America

Library of Congress Cataloging in Publication Data
Gilbert, Judy B. (Judy Bogen)
Clear speech.
Bibliography: p.
1. English language – Study and teaching – Foreign
speakers. 2. English language – United States –
Pronunciation. I. Title.
PE1128.A2G5   1984   428.3'4   83-15416

ISBN 0 521 28790 1 (Student's Book)
ISBN 0 521 28791 X (Teacher's Manual)
ISBN 0 521 24570 2 (Cassette)

Contents

Contents

Acknowledgments

I am grateful to the following field-test directors and teachers, who, by analyzing their field-test experiences, made the final version of this book more teachable:

People's Republic of China: (Chinese Academy of Sciences) Cameron Beatty, Breck Hill, Marsha Chan, Margaret van Naerssen

The Netherlands: (Catholic University, Nijmegen) Kees de Bot

Japan: (Aoyama School, Tokyo) Jon Fernald

Kuwait: (Kuwait University) W. James Griswold

U. S.: (California State University, San Francisco) Bob Benson, Rita Wong; (Cañada College) Yolanda Boykin; (Columbia University) Diana Berkowitz, Thaddeus Ferguson, Lou Levi, Margaret Shute; (De Anza College) Barbara Chan, Deena Levine; (East San Diego Adult Center) Darlene Elwin; (Stanford University) Chris Ely, Alice Stiebel; (University of California, Davis: English Department) Viola Peters, Tippy Schwabe, (Extension) Wanda Daley, Beryl Duffin, Rebecca Ford, Bourgie Hoerner, Ingrid Lusebrink, Janet Clare; (University of the Pacific) Carolyn Clark

Judy B. Gilbert

Cover design by Frederick Charles Ltd.
Book design by Peter Ducker

Cassette production by The Sun Group

Introduction

Here is a sad story: The teacher has just completed a successful pronunciation lesson using minimal pairs of words to teach the sounds "r" and "l." All of the students were able to manage the distinction by the end of the lesson. The students feel good and the teacher feels good. Then, as the students are leaving the room, one turns to the teacher and says cheerily, "So rong!" The teacher does not feel so good any more.

The fact is, minimal pair practice alone sometimes seems to yield minimal results. This may be part of the reason the teaching of pronunciation has fallen into disfavor in so many programs. Lack of success is discouraging to teachers, and students sometimes feel that pronunciation is an endless succession of unrelated and unmanageable pieces. If the work is so discouraging, shouldn't we just drop it? Why should we include pronunciation in the curriculum?

There are two main reasons to teach pronunciation: Students need to understand and to be understood. If they cannot hear English well, they are cut off from the language, except in printed form. If they cannot be understood easily, they are cut off from conversation with native speakers.

Pronunciation and listening comprehension are linked together. Furthermore, they are linked by a unified system within which the individual sounds are systematically related. Students need this sense of system, in order to make sense of the separate pieces.

Conscientious teachers ask, "How can we reduce student errors?" It can be more useful to turn that question around this way: "How can we increase student clarity?" This course is designed to help you achieve this goal.

Linguistic framework

Linguists generally refer to individual sounds as "segmentals." They use the term "suprasegmentals" to refer to patterns extending over a number of segmentals: for example, intonation. In most pronunciation textbooks, these two concepts, segmental and suprasegmental, are reflected in a decidedly lopsided way. Although there is almost invariably some brief description of intonation, the bulk of the text is generally devoted to the practice of individual sounds. This common imbalance comes from a tradition among linguists in which analysis is mostly concentrated on the segmentals. A distinguished dissenter from this tradition wrote that the musical part of speech, which comes first to a child, seems to come last to a linguist. He added, referring to intonation and rhythm: "If the child could paint the picture, these would be the wave on which the other components ride up and down; but the linguist is older and

1

stronger, and has his way – he calls them suprasegmentals, and makes the wave ride on top of the ship" (Bolinger 1961).

This textbook is based on the principle that intonation is the framework within which speech flows most clearly from speaker to listener. Practice with individual sounds is placed in a subordinate position, after practice with intonation. The sounds selected for practice are the most common problem sounds for most ESL students.

Sequence

In order to make this book manageable in the time allowed for an average class, some areas of pronunciation, although interesting and useful, have had to be treated briefly or not at all. The book concentrates on those areas most critical to clear speech. The sequencing is designed for general use, but you may find that a different order would be best for your particular class. For instance, if your students are already in a position where they must give an oral presentation (as teaching assistants or in seminars), you might find it useful to begin with Unit 32. The lecture in this unit discusses techniques that can compensate for pronunciation difficulties, thereby increasing clarity even before there is any direct work on pronunciation.

Transferring concepts to other class work

Practice in the identification of focus words is useful for both reading and composition classes. One reason for poor reading comprehension is the failure to notice linking or contrastive relationships between sentences. Relatively dull grammar drills can be enlivened by asking students which words might reflect new information: that is, which words should be emphasized when the drill is spoken aloud.

Self-analysis

Students should be encouraged to take dictation on the blackboard as much as possible, because this helps them recognize errors instantly. The self-analysis exercises can be done at home, in the lab, or in class, depending on time and the facilities available. Students generally find class recording useful, as soon as they get over their uneasiness at hearing their own recorded voices. Not all students need to be recorded at every class meeting, but each student should get an opportunity to do so during the semester, if possible. If classroom recording is not feasible, they should be encouraged to do this on their own. "Self-monitoring" is a necessary part of improvement.

Preparation for TOEFL

Many students are so worried about the TOEFL that they are reluctant to spend class time on pronunciation, because they do not see how it will help their score on the examination. You can assure them that work in this course can not only help them in the listening comprehension part of TOEFL (one-third of the test) but can also help develop reading skills, which are another major part of the examination. This is a reasonable promise, since learning to recognize the function of focus words is fundamentally related to language comprehension, spoken or written.

Lectures

Several short talks and lectures are included in the Listening section of the Student's Book. They are carefully sequenced, so that the first exercises are short and the later ones are longer. The comprehension tasks involve listening to and writing numbers, following directions, and finding places on a map. Some of the short talks can be used as dictations; the longer lectures are designed to help students learn to take notes as they listen, in preparation for university work. Two of the lectures are followed by multiple choice questions similar to those in the TOEFL.

Most of the material in the Listening section is recorded on the Cassette, and the transcripts appear at the back of the Student's Book. You can play the Cassette or read the lectures aloud. Students can have further practice by reading the transcripts aloud to one another in pairs or small groups.

Quizzes

There are two purposes for the quizzes included in this Teacher's Manual: (1) they motivate further practice, since students usually miss a few answers on each quiz, and (2) they eventually give you a profile of the students' listening weaknesses, which, in turn, is likely to be a good profile of pronunciation weaknesses. The quizzes can be photocopied and distributed in class as required. The answers are grouped together in one section and follow the quizzes.

Field testing

The explanations and comments in this manual were developed as the result of field testing by twenty-five teachers, all of whom had different backgrounds and teaching situations. Many of the practical suggestions came directly from the field-test teachers. Some of the problems discussed may never occur in your class, just as some of the material in the text will fit your particular situation better than will other parts of the book.

Use of the Cassettes

The Cassette symbol ▭ precedes material in the Student's Book that is recorded on the two accompanying Cassettes. Play the Cassettes or read the exercise aloud for listed exercises. If the exercise is not on the Cassette, you can read the material aloud. Students can also use the Cassettes individually for self-study and in the language laboratory.

Symbols used in the text

Slashes identify reduced vowels.

Example: bánaná

Parentheses signal reduction of the letter "h."

Example: Is (h)e busy? (sounds like "Izzybizzy?")

Rising and falling lines indicate the pitch of words and sentences.

Example: eleven   Is she there?

Bars and dots identify long and short syllables.

Example: record (noun)   record (verb)

Capital letters indicate stress.

Example: I WANT a baNAna.

Clear Listening Test

The Clear Listening Test appears on p. 3 of the Student's Book. You can either play the recording of the Clear Listening Test or read the appropriate parts by using the answer key that follows. It is helpful to give a test at the beginning of the course, to show the students what they may need to improve, and again later, to give an objective measure of progress.

When you score this test, be strict. The purpose is to alert the students to a need for improvement, so that they will pay attention to the following lessons. Students must learn to be sensitive to which syllable gets the stress if they wish to speak clearly, so it is a mistake to allow vague answers on this test. For instance, if the student correctly identified the direction of a pitch change but placed it on the wrong syllable, or vaguely included two or more syllables in underlining stress, take off a point.

Clear Listening Test: answers

Part 1: Stressed syllables (10 points)

1. parti̲cipating
2. pho̲tograph
3. photo̲graphy
4. alter̲native
5. uni̲versity

Part 2: Vowel clarity (10 points)

1. bánaná
2. Nébraská
3. womán
4. womén
5. Americá (accept either Americá or Americá)

Part 3: Voicing and length of syllable (10 points)

1a. What kind of word is "use"?	(noun)	—
b. What kind of word is "use"?	(verb)	✓
2a. He said "prove."	(verb)	—
b. He said "proof."	(noun)	✓
3a. What does "loose" mean?	(adjective)	—
b. What does "lose" mean?	(verb)	✓
4a. What kind of cap was it?		—
b. What kind of cab was it?		✓
5a. What's the prize?		✓
b. What's the price?		—

Part 4: Pitch patterns – words (10 points)

1. Barbara   3. Jonathan   5. Victor

2. Corinne   4. Elizabeth

Part 5: Pitch patterns – sentences (10 points)

1. It was awful!   4. This is my notebook.

2. She left her book.   5. This is my notebook.

3. She left her book?

Part 6: Contractions, reductions (10 points)

1. She doesn't <u>want to</u> study now.
2. Please <u>give him</u> the information. (accept <u>them</u> but not <u>me</u>)
3. <u>Do you</u> think she'll win?
4. <u>Where'll you</u> go?
5. How <u>long've</u> you been here?
6. <u>Is he</u> busy?
7. <u>Where's a</u> store?
8. Did <u>he go</u> to the concert?
9. <u>What's she</u> done?
10. Is <u>her work</u> good?

Part 7: Focus words (20 points)

A: What's the <u>matter</u>?
B: I lost my <u>hat</u>.
A: What <u>kind</u> of hat?
B: It was a <u>rain</u> hat.
A: What <u>color</u> rain hat?
B: It was <u>white</u>. White with <u>stripes</u>.
A: There <u>was</u> a white hat with stripes in the <u>car</u>.
B: <u>Which</u> car?
A: The one I <u>sold</u>.

Count off for every word underlined that is not the most important word.

Part 8: Thought groups (10 points)

1a. He sold his houseboat and trailer.   —

b. He sold his house, boat, and trailer.   ✓

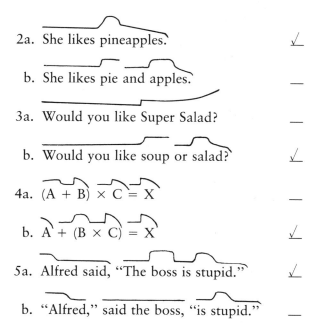

2a. She likes pineapples.   ✓

 b. She likes pie and apples.   —

3a. Would you like Super Salad?   —

 b. Would you like soup or salad?   ✓

4a. $(A + B) \times C = X$ —

 b. $A + (B \times C) = X$ ✓

5a. Alfred said, "The boss is stupid."   ✓

 b. "Alfred," said the boss, "is stupid."   —

The re-test should come after Unit 23, before the book turns to general listening comprehension. In order to get the best possible improvement of class scores, you should review the important points before giving the test. A quick way to do this is to put some words on the board and ask the class the number of syllables, which syllable is stressed, which has the pitch change, and which vowels are full. If you do this kind of quick review periodically and use frequent dictation, the class should do well on the re-test.

SYLLABLE UNITS

Unit 1 • Syllables

Unit 1 is long because it lays an essential foundation. The notes for this unit are especially detailed, since many of the points are also useful for later units.
  Syllable-sensitivity is important because:

1. It helps students identify the exact syllable for stress marking, which the native speaker relies on for clear understanding.
2. It helps students notice reduced syllables, such as articles, auxiliaries, and grammatical endings. These are often missing from students' speech (example: "Where is post office?"...*wrong*).

Play the Cassette or read the lists of words first vertically, then in random order. The students should tap their hands on their desks to count the syllables. Then call on individuals to tell how many syllables are in a given word.

| B |

The students' names can cause disagreement, which should be treated lightly. This is not an exact count exercise. Caution: Japanese de-voices the vowels "ee" (as in "eat") and "u" (as in "boot") between voiceless consonants or between a voiceless consonant and silence (as at the end of a word). Therefore, a Japanese version of the name Hiroshi or Yoshiko is apt to sound like two syllables. Do not allow yourself or the class to get tangled in argument, but just move on to the next name.

  Another problem you may run into with Japanese students is that they count nasals ("n," "m," "ng") as syllables, with the result that a word like "insutanto" (the Japanese version of "instant") will sound like a six syllable word to a Japanese! You can explain that an English syllable needs a vowel in the center of the syllable. The most practical solution to this and other confusions is to use tapping exercises until students intuitively perceive syllables in an English sense.

  Despite what would appear to be a worrisome variety of reasons for people not to get the point right away, most students do pick up the idea of syllables rapidly. The concept is repeated regularly in the following units.

  A nice addition to this exercise is to have the students spell their names to you as you write them on the blackboard. This is a useful check of alphabet control. At moments of communication difficulty, it is helpful to be able to spell clearly, but a surprising number of advanced students are not able to say all letters of the alphabet correctly. Common errors are with the letters "i," "e," "g," "j." Unless the control is automatic, spelling the problem word will just compound the communication difficulty. This is the time for students to discover alphabet weaknesses. The exercise also has the advantages of introducing the class members to each other and helping you to learn their names quickly.

Answers for column 3:

academic	4	classification	5
sentences	3	economy	4
registration	4	economical	5
international	5		

Here are some cross-language comparisons of syllable number that you can put on the board. This is an enlightening exercise for some students.

Spanish/English	*Japanese/English*	*Arabic/English*
clase/class	terebi//TV	lamba/lamp
chocolate/chocolate	miruku/milk	kimie/chemistry

English: cocoa (2)   *German*: Kakao (2)

                           Japanese: kokoa (3)

          hygiene (2)   *Russian*: gigiena (4)

          French (1)   *French*: Français (2)

          chocolate (2)   *German*: Schokolade (4)

                    Spanish: chocolate (4)

Chocolate is such a common loan word that many of your students may be able to supply a version from their languages. The comparison words given here are meant as rough examples. Your students may spell these words differently or even pronounce them differently, because of dialect variations, but the comparisons can be quite helpful.

Some of your students may speak languages that do not normally have consonants at the end of words. They may feel the teacher is simply being fussy in reminding them to pay attention to final consonants. This exercise and F can help motivate students to sharpen their final consonants, by making clear the grammatical significance of their presence or absence.

Answers:

painted	2	rented	2	added	2	caused	1
crowded	2	worked	1	faded	2	filled	1
walked	1	laughed	1	watched	1	closed	1

Students can practice alternate endings in pairs: One student says "dishes" and the other student says "dish." Words should be selected at random so that students won't simply answer mechanically without listening.

You can play the Cassette or you can read both sentences and ask if the class heard a "wrong sentence" or a "right sentence." If the class seems relaxed, they can then be asked to test each other. You may feel uneasy asking students to say incorrect sentences. The advantage of doing it is that they may be able to focus better when asked to "feel" the error personally.

Answers (use these choices or choose your own):

1. The ice is cold.   right
2. Her dress pretty.   wrong
3. The bus late.   wrong
4. The bus are late.   wrong
5. He washes dishes.   right
6. He needed a bike.   right
7. She visit her sister.   wrong
8. The river flooded the valley.   right
9. This book was print with ink.   wrong
10. Yesterday we rent an apartment.   wrong

I

Dictation:

1. They've already <u>painted</u> the apartment for her.
2. He didn't really <u>need</u> that much money.
3. She's trying to <u>learn</u> everything.
4. We've just <u>started</u> to learn irregular verbs.
5. You'll need two more <u>boxes</u> for all those <u>dresses</u>.
6. <u>She packed her dress and blouses in the suitcase.</u> (11)
7. <u>The buses arrived at six o'clock.</u> (9)
8. <u>They wanted to rent an apartment.</u> (9)
9. <u>They rented it the day before yesterday.</u> (11)

After the dictation, ask the class to report the total number of syllables of the last four sentences. They are likely to be surprised by the correct number. Tap out the syllables, if necessary.

In sentence 6, check the number of syllables for "dress" and "blouses." Spelling is not important here; however the word is spelled, the student should be able to read it aloud with the correct number of syllables.

In sentence 8, the critical question is the tense of "wanted." It is followed by a reduced syllable "to," making it difficult to hear correctly.

In sentence 9, "rented it the" has three reduced syllables in a row. Sensitivity to the rhythm of these three short syllables will help the listener recognize the presence of the pronoun and article, which are so frequently omitted in students' speech and writing.

Self-analysis

The words "this is" may cause over-correction, with too much emphasis to a word, "is," that should normally be deemphasized. That possibility is justified at this point of the course because of the importance of getting students to "feel" the presence of a syllable. No matter how unstressed or short a syllable is, it must still be present.

WORD UNITS

Unit 2 • Stress: pitch

It has long been the practice to teach stress as if it were synonymous with loudness, but this approach may not be as useful as has been assumed. Loudness is used to indicate stress in most languages. What is new to students, and therefore more productive to teach, are the signals that are not used in their languages, or that are used in different combinations or for different functions. These are the three most powerful signals for indicating stress in English (Bolinger 1958; Fry 1955):

1. Pitch change
2. Length of vowel
3. Clarity of vowel

English speakers use pitch patterns to identify words, so ignoring this part of pronunciation is a serious error.

If you hum pitch patterns into a kazoo (a toy instrument that amplifies humming), the pitch changes will be very clear. When you get accustomed to using a kazoo, it is a useful tool for correcting mis-stressed words. It is an auditory image of an auditory fact. Drawing pitch lines is also an aid to concentration. It is not easy to learn to think about the direction of pitch change, so all kinds of kinesthetic aids (like pointing a hand up or down) can help focus attention.

$\boxed{\text{E}}$

Answers:

semester	admission
quarter	applicant
division	application
registration	education
enrollment	

$\boxed{\text{F}}$

Answers:

requirements   residence

graduate   degree

12

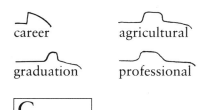

career   agricultural

graduation   professional

G

You can use the word *chocolate* again as a cross-language comparison. After
you write the different versions on the board (if you have a mixed-language
class), ask the students to tell you which syllable has the pitch change. Draw
the pitch line and ask if the class is satisfied that you got it right. Sometimes
students will get confused and give you the wrong pattern. However, when
you then pronounce the word as indicated on the board, all the people from
that language group will recognize an error. This kind of practice helps the
class to see that analyzing pitch patterns is quite difficult – they may at first
have assumed it was "too easy." It requires concentration even for a very familiar word from one's own language.

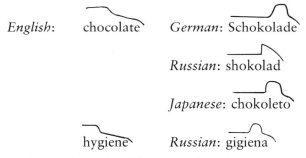

English: chocolate   *German*: Schokolade

Russian: shokolad

Japanese: chokoleto

hygiene   *Russian*: gigiena

The students should now realize that hearing pitch patterns in a new language is going to require paying attention during the practice in this lesson. It
is also useful to discover that a loan word may have a different pitch pattern
in a different language.

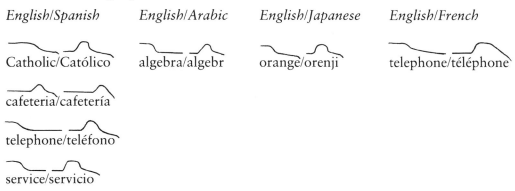

English/Spanish   *English/Arabic*   *English/Japanese*   *English/French*

Catholic/Católico   algebra/algebr   orange/orenji   telephone/téléphone

cafeteria/cafetería

telephone/teléfono

service/servicio

If your students come from tone language backgrounds (Thai, Chinese, Vietnamese, among others), be prepared for a more complicated pitch line, since
each syllable will have its own pattern.

Some teachers may object that this "contrastive analysis" is taking time
away from practicing the new language. Unlike children, who learn pronunci-

ation well by mimicry, adults can be helped by learning to be alert to the ways each language varies the use of universal elements like pitch. It is also helpful to students to realize that pronunciation is systematic. The mispronunciation of their names by Americans is not due to indifference or hostility, but simply to the systematic application of English rules.

Sample names:

Japanese/English   *Spanish/English*

Yasumasa/Yasumasa   Mañuel/Manuel

The contrast between teens and tens can be taught as a fixed pattern:

fifteen   fifty
thirteen   thirty

The numbers 13–19 are usually spoken with this stress pattern. However, pressure from sentence rhythm and intonation, due to the emphasis of important words, can alter the usual pitch pattern of any word. Most of the time, though, words are stressed in sentences according to their dictionary stress patterns.

H

Answers:

1. James, Jim, Jimmy   1. Elizabeth, Beth, Betty

2. William, Bill, Billy   2. Patricia, Pat, Patty

3. Robert, Bob, Bobby   3. Susan, Sue, Suzie

I

Dictation:

1. He's studying economics.
2. They've decided to eat in a new restaurant.
3. That woman's name is Elizabeth.
4. His name is Thomas, but everyone calls him Tommy.
5. We're learning to hear American pitch patterns.

Self-analysis

If you have a tape recorder that has different speeds, you can play back the recording at a slower than normal speed. This makes the pitch changes easier to notice.

Homework: Ask students to bring three English words, marked for pitch patterns. They can write them on the board, with pitch lines, or dictate them to you to write. The class can then judge the accuracy of the analysis.

Unit 3 • Stress: length

In some languages, vowel length makes a difference in meaning, in the same way that "bit" and "bet" are different words in English.

Japanese example: oba-san = aunt

obaa-san = grandmother

For native speakers of such a language, it is easy to hear vowel length differences but hard to associate this length with stress, which is its basic function in English.

A

Use students' names again. A long name, like Yasumasa, is especially good for demonstrating the uneven length of syllables that is characteristic of English. First get the student to demonstrate the pitch pattern of his or her name:

Yasumasa

Now you can show how Americans typically place a pitch rise on the next-to-last syllable in an unknown word (abracaDAbra). Because pitch change and length are tied together in English (unlike many languages), the whole rhythmic pattern is altered:

Yasumasa   Yasumasa   (English version)

B

The words in column 2 should take longer than the words in column 1 because they end in a vowel and are therefore much longer than the words that end in "p," "t," or "k" (unvoiced stops make the preceding vowel shorter; see Unit 19). This exercise is helpful for students who tend to drop final consonants, since it alerts them to this distinction.

Stretching wide, heavy rubber bands while practicing the lengthened vowels can provide students with a kinesthetic focusing tool to reinforce the contrast in this and subsequent duration-contrast exercises. Some teachers demonstrate with rubber gloves, large (unblown) balloons, or elasticized fabric. Students can test the class by saying "Did I say ____ or ____?"

Ask students to *whisper* a few of these contrasts, in order to focus their attention on length rather than pitch. After practicing these sets, go back to Unit 2, D, to show how length and pitch change go together. By this time the students should have a much clearer understanding of why Americans mispronounce their names or other words from their language. The next unit (vowel clarity) should complete the picture.

Answers:

extend	wider	require
inform	over	gather
arrive	campus	unit

F

Dictation:

1. Oh, did you lose something?
2. Pack the dresses into the suitcase.
3. I think this handle is loose.
4. What can I use to fix a broken handle?
5. They haven't loaded our baggage yet.

   Besides stress, which affects vowel length at the level of the syllable (further developed in Unit 7), there are lengthening effects at the level of the sentence. Because English depends so much on stress to highlight the important words in a sentence (see Unit 12), length affects more than just syllable rhythm. Because these different uses of length are likely to be new concepts for students, they should be taught one at a time. This Unit is important because it is the foundation for later concepts.

Unit 4 • Stress: clarity

It ought to come as good news to the students that they do not have to pronounce every sound clearly. In fact, they should not.

   Conscientious teachers tend to enunciate every sound clearly, in order to help their students understand. They pronounce the unstressed syllables just as clearly as the stressed syllables. In fact, this is a kind of English that native English speakers use *only* when talking to foreigners. The unfortunate effect of using such a model of spoken English is that, as Gillian Brown has said, students find it quite impossible to understand normal spoken English. They do not learn to rely on structural information given them by the rhythm of speech but rely instead upon clear and distinct pronunciations of all vowels and consonants. [Brown 1977, p. 46]

Later lessons will deal with clarity of the consonants in stressed syllables. At this point the student's attention must be drawn only to the contrast between clarity and reduction in the vowels.

Most languages are very careful to preserve the sound of each vowel in its full form. This makes the English vowel reduction system very foreign to most English learners. If English is spoken with all vowels full, stress patterns become confused for English listeners. One technique is to say a word with all the vowels in full form, then with correct combinations of full and reduced vowels. The student can practice saying the word both ways, to feel the difference.

Additional activities can be helpful:

1. You can use *chocolate* again as an additional example. In most languages every vowel will be full. In English, the second vowel is either reduced or completely missing. The students' names can also be analyzed from the perspective of vowel clarity:

Typical American pronunciation

Yasúmasá Házamá   Máriá Ortegá-Cárillo   Múhammád Nájjar

2. Write "woman/women" on the board. Ask the students which vowel sound changes, the first or the second. At least some students are likely to say the second. Now remind them that you asked about the vowel *sound*, not the spelling. Ask them to use their ears, not their eyes, and to listen for the difference between full vowels and reduced vowels. Say the words again several times. Despite the spelling, the second vowel sounds roughly the same in each case. This is the *shwa* (or *schwa*) sound, and it is probably the most common sound in English.

Answers:

printéd	limít
landéd	watchés
dramá	rentéd
meltéd	finísh
bottóm	messés

After you have practiced the exercises contrasting clear vowels and unclear vowels, point out that the words "the" and "a" are spoken differently, according to whether they are followed by a vowel or a consonant:

thé plum	the apple
thé pear	the orange
thé decision	the election

F

Answers:

campus	professor (or professor)	photograph
college	seminar	photography
degree	registration	semester

G

Dictation:

1. There's always an <u>examination</u> at the end of the <u>preparation</u>.
2. We <u>visited</u> three states: <u>Alaska</u>, <u>Alabama</u>, and <u>Oklahoma</u>.
3. She's going to <u>visit</u> two places: <u>Arabia</u> and <u>Brazil</u>.
4. You've got to spend <u>a lot</u> of time in <u>preparing</u> for any profession.
5. <u>Reduced</u> vowels are never <u>stressed</u>.

Unit 5 • Review

Syllables

Answers (there is an asterisk after each word with an added syllable):

added*	proposes*	wanted*	wiped
caused	pointed*	poses*	recommended*
shouted*	developed	mixes*	mixed
checked	announces*	attached	advances*
advanced	happens	wasted*	opposes*
happened	avoided*	described	acted*

Pitch patterns

Tom   Jeanie   Anthony   Ellen

Jerome   Victoria   Elaine

Unit 6 • Stress patterns

Many students assume that word stress patterns are some sort of frill, or else they do not notice them at all. An English teacher from Colombia reported that one of her students returned home from university work in the United States with a complaint. He reported angrily that he had many times told people that his study major was "eCOnomics," but that "they pretended not to understand."

Far from being frills, stress patterns are an essential part of the pronunciation of English words. There is some research evidence suggesting that native speakers store vocabulary according to stress patterns. When the wrong pattern is heard, the listener may spend time searching stored words in the wrong category. By the time the listener realizes something is wrong, the original sequence of sounds may be forgotten. For this reason, a stress pattern mistake can cause great confusion.

A multisyllabic word will have more than one stressed syllable (Abraca-DAbra, AcaDEmic). These stresses are usually described as the primary stress (main) and the secondary stress (lesser). For practical teaching purposes, it is enough that the student be able to recognize the main, or primary, stress.

There is no real need for the students to understand the meaning of the word used in the example:

MIcrocónTAmínánt

It is used simply to demonstrate the principle of noticing the stress pattern of a new word. However, if the class really wants to know, you can say that "micro" means small and "contaminant" means pollutant, or something like dirt, so the word refers to a kind of dirt small enough to be seen only under a microscope. In general, it is better not to be led into vocabulary discussion, because that is something students can do by themselves with a dictionary at home.

C

Answers:

personality   pathogenic
mammalian   metabolic
analytical   calculus
pharmacology

D

Answers:

| 1. under over | S | 3. require offer | D |
| 2. question answer | S/S | 4. Alaska Nebraska | S/S |

5. corr<u>ec</u>tion <u>in</u>stitute   D
6. cert<u>i</u>ficate d<u>e</u>livery   S
7. cons<u>i</u>derably manu<u>fac</u>turer D

8. <u>ab</u>solu<u>te</u>ly re<u>co</u>very   D
9. ex<u>pen</u>sive re<u>quire</u>ment   S
10. <u>spe</u>cify <u>se</u>parate   S

E

If the class is absorbing the principle of word stress patterns well, this might be a good time to alert them to the difference between words that form a phrase and words that form a single unit, like compound nouns (black board / blackboard). One of the examples most often used to show this difference is the pair "lighthouse keeper/light housekeeper." The definition of "light housekeeping" usually refers to the person's weight, but Edna Ferber had this to say about a housemaid, who was a lighthouse keeper's daughter: "Housekeeping in that home must be light housekeeping indeed, for the housemaid's ideas on cleaning are airy to the point of non-existence" (*A Peculiar Treasure*, 1960, p.

You can practice the following pairs to further sensitize students to the way English uses stress to show meaning (the students do not need to memorize these pairs):

black bird	blackbird	(a particular type of bird)
white house	White House	(the home of the U.S. president)
green house	greenhouse	(a special building for growing plants)
blue book	Blue Book	(the examination booklet used for university examinations in the U.S.)

Prator and Robinett (1972, p. 20) give some rough rules for the stress pattern of compounds.

1. Compound *nouns* generally have the stress on the first part. (drugstore, thoroughfare, weatherman)
2. Compound *verbs* generally have the stress on the second part. (understand, overlook, outrun)

These rules fit well with the stress patterns for two-word verbs in Unit 6, p. 25. There seems to be a general "verbness" about stressing the second part.

Note: All of these patterns can be overridden by the needs of sentence emphasis. That is because the English speaker uses sentence accents to make the most important words more easily noticeable. If these accents are too close together, they tend to detract from each other's importance. For that reason, English speakers have a tendency to separate these accents by shifting the normal stress:

There are thirTEEN of them.
THIRteen MEN and THIRteen WOmen.

Warning: These rules for phrase stress are fine for a class that is managing the basic material well. But if the students are under some strain already, this extra amount of information could be fatal to enthusiasm. Students can proceed with confidence if the learning burden is within their capacity. Only you can judge the capacity of your own class.

G

Dictation

1. He's got to look out when he talks to his boss.
2. We've often gone up to that lookout.
3 Do you think she's going to be upset with us?
4. It's important to turn off the motor when you're waiting in the car.

Unit 7 • English rhythm

Rhythm in English is not just something extra, added to the basic sequence of conso-nants and vowels, it is the guide to the structure of information in the spoken mes-sage. [Brown 1977, p. 43]

The most important feature of English rhythm is that the syllables are not equal in duration. In crude terms, there are three lengths for vowels (the cen-ters of syllables):

1. Reduced (sofá)
2. Full vowel unstressed (alteRAtion)
3. Full vowel stressed (alteRAtion)

A peculiar characteristic of English is that there is a fourth length: When two full vowels are said in succession, they become longer. To be more exact, the full vowel preceding another full vowel becomes longer. For practical pur-poses, it is enough to say that full vowels get lengthened when they are said in succession.

These vowel lengths are not exact measurements, so there is no point in trying to reduce English to musical notation or in asking students to practice three-way or four-way timing contrasts. The purpose of this lesson is simply to increase their alertness to the irregularity of English syllables and to make them aware of the general principle that length adds emphasis. The sign at the zoo saying DON'T FEED BEARS has more "command power" than it would with an article before "bears," because of the succession of full vowels.

It is this irregularity of syllable length that makes it difficult to make a musically satisfying translation of poetry, when going from a regular-syllable language (like Spanish, Japanese, Tagalog, and others) to an irregular-syllable language (like English, German, or French) or vice versa.[1] It is a basic cause of "foreign accent" in English.

[1]It is more accurate to make a distinction between regular syllable languages and irregular syllable languages than to distinguish between the concept of syllable timing versus stress timing (Bolinger 1981).

English rhythm is based not only on varying syllable lengths but on sentence emphasis effects. The two levels (syllable timing and sentence accents) are very different. The following explanation comes from a letter from Dwight L. Bolinger, Professor of Romance Languages and Literature Emeritus, Harvard University:

To take the example I am most familiar with, English and Spanish behave in almost exactly the same way as far as accentual rhythm is concerned, and yet we know that the rhythmic impression they make is quite different. That difference lies at the level of syllabic rhythm, and the main component of the difference is the thing that is keyed to vowel reduction, namely the extra length that is conditioned by successive unreduced syllables.

Answers:

1. Go tell Grace. (all full)
2. Go ánd tell ít tó Grace. (different lengths)
3. Give hím á pencíl. (different lengths)
4. Those young men work hard. (all full)
5. All thé womén áre workíng. (different lengths)
6. Soap gets out dirt fast. (all full)
7. All soap makes clothes clean. (all full)
8. Thé soap wíll clean yóúr jackét. (different lengths)
9. Maný Englísh vowéls áre quite short ín real speech. (different lengths)
10. Planes use airports. (all full)

Limericks are used in this book to take advantage of the way the swing of the rhythm forces reductions and contractions. This rhythmic swing will be broken if the students have to pause at each line to figure out which word to emphasize. It is better to have them read the limerick first to themselves and underline the emphasized words before oral practice. By beginning with a choral reading, no individual is put on the spot. Each half of the class can alternate taking lines. If the teacher acts as a choral leader, clapping a strong rhythmic pattern (or thumping a hand on the table), the class will stay together in a satisfying way. Without this leadership, the rhythm is apt to become uncertain, which makes students uneasy.

One alternative technique for any rhythm practice is to *whisper* it. This concentrates the mind on timing rather than pitch patterns.

Further rhythm practice possibilities:

(a) The song "All I want for Christmas is my two front teeth" is good for a class where no one's religious feeling is apt to be disturbed. The final three words are emphatic, because of a succession of full vowels. Any song or poem that you like can demonstrate variation caused by full and reduced vowels. Carolyn Graham's *Jazz Chants* is a good source for rhythm practice.

(b) Practice saying the verses of the following spiritual, slowing down dramatically for the succession of full vowels in "whole world." ("Little bitty baby" takes about the same length of time as "whole world" when this song is sung.)

He's Got the Whole World in His Hands

1. He's got the whole world in His hands (4 times)

2. He's got the little bitty baby in His hands (3 times)
   He's got the whole world, in His hands.

3. He's got you 'n me, sister, in His hands (3 times)
   He's got the whole world in His hands.

THOUGHT UNITS
Unit 9 • Reductions

There are many kinds of reduction in English, but reduction of pronouns and auxiliaries may be the most important because they are so common and cause so much comprehension difficulty. Although the principle of contraction and pronoun reduction is fairly easy to understand, it is not at all easy to acquire the habit of recognizing these words in spoken English.

   It is not necessary for students to use these reductions in their own speech. In fact, it is better if they speak slowly when they really need to be understood, and these reductions sound peculiar in slow speech. However, it is useful for them to practice saying the reductions, because this practice can help them hear spoken English better.

A

Have students test each other, either testing the whole group or (better) in pairs: "Did I say *a* or *b*?" Answers:

1. Did he go?   (a)
2. Is she here?   (b)
3. Give her the book.   (b)
4. Send him the pen.   (a)
5. Is our work good?   (b)

C

In sentence 8 it is also possible to reduce the pronoun "he."

D

Answers:

1. Do you think he ̶has gone?
2. Where ̶have they been?
3. How long ̶have you been here?
4. I have to do some work now.
5. Do you think she ̶has gone yet?
6. University students have to work hard.
7. You ̶have done enough.
8. He has six classes.

E

Dictation:

1. We hope <u>he's</u> ready to go.
2. Did they say <u>they're</u> coming?

3. That's what <u>they're</u> doing.
4. I said <u>I'm</u> going to do it.
5. We think <u>you've</u> done enough.

Answers:

1. No, I do not think she has.
2. Yes, I have.
3. I think you are.
4. Maybe they will.
5. He *is* sure that they will bring some.
6. He *is* sure that they will.

Dictation:

1. Give (h)im the information.
2. Why did (h)e ask that?

3. Do you think they've gone yet?
4. Where did (h)e go?
5. I'm afraid that (h)er dog bit (h)im.

6. We've listened very carefully.
7. If I'd known about the party I'd (h)ave come.
8. This (h)as been a good class.
9. The train (h)as come.
10. The train's here.

One way to reinforce this lesson is to have students check each other's dictation. Another technique is to have students check their own dictation and then report their errors, which you can tally on the board. This gives a focused moment to practice saying and hearing the correct forms.

If the class is in a low mood (middle of the semester, too much rain, etc.), you can provide a change of pace with Vanishing Letters: Give each student a piece of clear red plastic (a report cover can be cut into 8 pieces) and a red pencil (half a pencil is adequate). Ask them to write sentences from this lesson in regular pencil or pen on a sheet of paper but to substitute the red pencil for all silent "h" letters. The red pencil must be pressed very lightly for this game to work. Demonstrate with chalk on the board. When they put the red plastic over their writing, they will have a read-aloud script with blank spaces to remind them of the existence of the reduced "h" letters. This technique uses both the concentration required to stop and change pencils, and the visual image of the blank space, to focus attention on the point being learned. The physical effort of changing pencils and writing lightly is added to mental recognition.

If you collect the Vanishing Letters equipment, you can use it another day for the following activity: Divide the class into small groups. Write a few words with silent letters on the board (island, knife, walk). Tell the groups that they have five minutes to think of as many such words as possible. At the end of five minutes, a reporter from each group should write their words on the board. People generally think of these words in patterns (light, right, might, etc.), which organize the words into sets for good practice. Have everybody copy the whole list, switching pencils for the silent letters. Then, with a red filter over the list, they can take turns reading aloud. If a student has not been alert while writing the list, the filtered script will not blank out the silent letters.

As you circulate among the teams during their five-minute group work, you can offer the following words to any team that seems stuck:

could (would, should, etc.)   comb, bomb
ought (bought, thought, etc.)   knife, knee, knock, know
Wednesday   sign, muscle, subtle
hour, honest

Unit 10 • Basic emphasis pattern

Ignorance of the basic pattern of English emphasis not only adds an element of confusion to the student's speech, but it also means the student is missing important signals in listening comprehension.

The distinction between content word and structure word is a universal part of human speech, but few people are consciously aware of these categories. You can help students become aware of the difference by asking them what kind of words they would put in a telegram. If they have to pay for every word, they will naturally choose the words that carry the most information. These are generally the content words. Another rough way to think about the difference is to describe content words as "picture words." You can visualize "book," "green," and "run," but no picture is likely to come to mind for words like "is," "the," or "if."

You can make a game of telegram writing: Give students a sentence and tell them they must convey the message in only three words. Example:

We need the report on Wednesday.   Need report Wednesday.

You can help Japanese students recognize the difference between content words and structure words by mentioning the difference between the *kana* and the *kanji* characters in written Japanese. The kana (characters representing syllable sounds) are generally used to "spell" structure words. The kanji (characters representing whole ideas) are generally used to convey content words.

One good way to illustrate emphasis is to bring a highlighter pen to class. American students use these pens to mark printed material that they study. The highlighted words are likely to be content words. "Highlight" is more or less synonymous with "emphasize."

Answers:

A <u>student</u> was <u>sent</u> to <u>Tacoma</u>
<u>intending</u> to <u>earn</u> a <u>diploma</u>.
He <u>said</u>, "With the <u>rain</u>,
I <u>don't</u> <u>want</u> to <u>remain</u>.
I <u>think</u> <u>I'd</u> <u>prefer</u> <u>Oklahoma</u>."

Many foreign students are suspicious of contractions, regarding them as substandard usage. This feeling can produce a covert resistance during exercises practicing contractions or reductions. It may be helpful for you to emphasize that contractions are not proper in formal *written* English but are a natural part of *spoken* educated English. The purpose of contraction and reduction is to downplay the less important words, in order to more fully highlight the important ones.

Answers:

1. Do you <u>like</u> the <u>picture</u> on your <u>passport</u>?
2. Did you <u>take</u> a <u>test</u> for a <u>driver's license</u> in this <u>country</u>?
3. <u>Students</u> <u>pay</u> a <u>lot</u> of <u>money</u> for their <u>books</u>, don't you <u>think</u>?
4. Do you <u>think</u> it is <u>harder</u> to <u>speak</u> or to <u>hear</u> a <u>foreign language</u>?
5. Is there a <u>speed limit</u> for <u>cars</u> in your <u>country</u>?

Self-analysis

X: What's the <u>matter</u>?
Y: I <u>lost</u> my <u>keys</u>.
X: Where'd you <u>put</u> them?
Y: If I <u>knew</u>, I could <u>find</u> them!

Unit 11 • Review

Reduction

Dictation:

1. When did (h)e ask you that?
2. I don't know what (h)e needs.
3. Did (h)e ask (h)er that?
4. She's asked for another class.
5. She would've told (h)im if she'd known.

Basic emphasis pattern

The <u>size</u> of the <u>state</u> of <u>Connecticut</u>
<u>affects</u> our <u>grammatical etiquette</u>.
To be <u>extra polite</u>,
a <u>Subject's</u> all <u>right</u>,
but the <u>space</u> is too <u>small</u> for a <u>Predicate</u>.

Unit 12 • Sentence focus (part 1)

Intonation is commonly thought of as having the following two functions:

1. Distinguishing sentence types, such as questions versus statements
2. Showing attitude

The first concept, though useful, does not go very far. On the simplest level, it is easily practiced but does not explain much. The second concept seems reasonable, but in practical classroom terms, it is vague and subject to bewildering variation.

A more useful approach is to concentrate on the *primary* functions of intonation (Daneš 1960):

1. Dividing speech into thought groups
2. Highlighting the focus of meaning

Emphasis on the focus word highlights the contrast between new and old information. All languages have one or more ways to show this difference, but English relies on intonation for this purpose more than most of our students' languages. For that reason, learning to hear this emphasis is both difficult and important. Students typically miss spoken signals of contrast with something said or assumed previously. When they learn to notice this intonation signal and recognize the implications, they make a major step forward in listening comprehension. As Virginia Allen has said:

Students (and sometimes teachers) ask: "But don't *all* languages use stress for signaling contrast and emphasis? Don't speakers of *all* languages call attention to a word by saying it more loudly than the words around it?" The point is, in most other languages there is far less *reduction* of stress on the surrounding words, with the result that those words compete with the stressed element for the (English) listener's attention. Try having a foreign student say: "Paris is not an American city; Paris is a French city." Unless he has developed an exceptional mastery of the English stress system, he will retain too much stress on both *Paris* and *city* in the second clause; he will fail to lower the stress on those words as English speakers do. [1971, p. 81]

B

Dialogue 1

A: Where are you GOING?
B: EUROPE.
A: WHERE in Europe? To the NORTH or to the SOUTH?
B: NEITHER. I've already BEEN north and south. I'm going EAST.

Dialogue 2

X: What've you been DOING?
Y: I've been STUDYING.
X: Studying WHAT? MATH or ENGLISH?

28

Y: NEITHER. I'm SICK of math and English. I'm studying NUTRITION, because I'm always HUNGRY.

Answers:

4. This is <u>my</u> book.   No, it's <u>his</u> book.
5. She wrote that <u>article</u>.   No, <u>I</u> wrote it.
6. Classes finish on the <u>sixteenth</u>.   No, I think they finish on the <u>fifteenth</u>.
7. The keys are on the <u>desk</u>.   No, they're <u>in</u> the desk.
8. He's speaking to <u>Marie</u>.   No, he's speaking <u>about</u> Marie.
9. They sell books in the <u>library</u>.   No, they sell books in the <u>bookstore</u>. They <u>lend</u> books in the library.
10. He can write <u>well</u>.   He <u>can</u>, but he <u>doesn't</u>. Too <u>lazy</u>.

   In item 6 above, notice that "fifteenth" has the stress on the first syllable, unlike its usual stress pattern. That is because the idea that must be contrasted is "fif." The need to show emphasis of a new idea overrides the stress pattern of the word.

Answers:

X: Do you think American food's <u>expensive</u>?
Y: Not <u>really</u>.
X: Well, <u>I</u> think it's expensive.
Y: That's because you eat in <u>restaurants</u>.
X: Where do <u>you</u> eat?
Y: At <u>home</u>.
X: I didn't know you could <u>cook</u>.
Y: Well, actually I <u>can't</u>. I just eat <u>bread</u> and <u>Coke</u>.
X: That's <u>awful</u>!
Y: No, it <u>isn't</u>. I <u>like</u> bread and Coke.
X: You're <u>crazy</u>!

Answers:

A: Hi! What's <u>new</u>?
B: <u>Nothing</u> much. What's new with <u>you</u>?
A: I'm going to <u>Washington</u>.
B: Washington <u>State</u> or Washington, <u>D.C.</u>?
A: <u>D.C.</u> I want to see the <u>capital</u>.

H

Answers:

1. When did you <u>arrive</u> here?

2. Where did you get your <u>English</u> book?
3. Who told you how to get a <u>visa</u>?
4. What <u>languages</u> can you <u>speak</u>?
5. Which language is the most <u>difficult</u> to learn?
6. Do you think it is harder to <u>speak</u> or to <u>hear</u> a foreign language?

Any short dialogue or skit can be used for focus word practice. A game that can help practice deemphasizing old information is the Alphabet Memory Game:

1st student: I went to New York and took an <u>apple</u>.
2nd student: I went to New York and took an apple and a <u>bicycle</u>.
3rd student: I went to New York and took an apple, a bicycle, and a <u>cat</u>.

Unit 13 • *The importance of focus*

This story can be read aloud by you or by the students. It can also be re-told as an exercise in sequencing events so that they are easy for the listener to follow ("What happened next?"). This is also part of clear speech.

However you choose to handle the lesson, students should have the opportunity to both hear and feel the physical differences between "He'll KILL us!" and HE'LL kill US!"

C

Answer: Earlier in the conversation the wife must have said something like "We'll KILL <u>him</u>!"

The turning point of the story, so easy for native speakers of English to understand, is apt to baffle many foreign students. This is because their languages do not use intonation as a means to contrast old and new information. One Japanese student reported that he had seen the movie *The Conversation* in Japan (with subtitles) but had not been able to understand it at all. Furthermore, he said that the movie played only briefly and puzzled all its Japanese audiences. The reason is simple: The subtitle could translate the meaning of the contrasting sentences only by using different word endings, which in Japanese show the shift in focus. Therefore the audience could not imagine why the detective should mis-hear the sentence, since the words were quite different. This same translation problem probably ruined the movie's run many places where it was subtitled in another language. The confusion is directly related to students' lack of awareness of the intonation signals of English.

If your students have trouble understanding the point about focus in this story, tell them that the two sentences differ in what they imply about the previous context. If a usually unemphasized word is emphasized, it implies a contrast with something said before.

Unit 14 • Sentence focus (part 2)

There are two simultaneous teaching points in this lesson:

1. The concept of focus words is extended into more complicated language use. It is extremely difficult but essential for students to begin to think of words not simply as they relate to sentences, but as they relate to the whole discourse structure. This exercise deals with written language; but the use of intonational highlighting, when these paragraphs are read aloud, is closely related to the way students should be reading for meaning when they read silently.
2. Many foreign students instinctively raise defenses against American culture, because they are afraid of being indoctrinated or changed in some way. These defenses can effectively bar learning the *style* of the culture, which is, in fact, necessary for clear communication in the new language. Students need to see that there is a practical advantage to becoming sensitive to cross-cultural style differences.

This quotation from E. M. Forster's *A Passage to India* expresses the need for teaching point 2: "A pause in the wrong place, an intonation misunderstood, and a whole conversation went awry." Unfortunately, people commonly mistake the intonation patterns of foreigners for insolence, indifference, or bad attitudes in general. Similarly, the politeness rules of one culture are often wrongly judged by people from another culture. For this reason, anyone wanting to do business of any kind in a foreign country will find practical advantage in learning some of the local rules.

A	B	C

Have the students read each paragraph and mark it, perhaps in pairs. Emphasize that people can have legitimate differences of opinion about the relative importance of words. The main point is simply to practice thinking about this relative importance and to overcome the widespread tendency to think word by word.

This lesson can be the basis for greatly increasing English effectiveness. Most students are trained to prepare for tests, an activity that concentrates their minds on *correctness*. This fixation on right versus wrong should not be allowed to overwhelm this lesson. Students need to learn to think about the possible intent of the speaker or writer. What does the speaker want the listener to notice? If the students can ask each other whether a word represents an old idea or a new idea, they are on the way to genuine comprehension.

Unit 15 • Questions

B

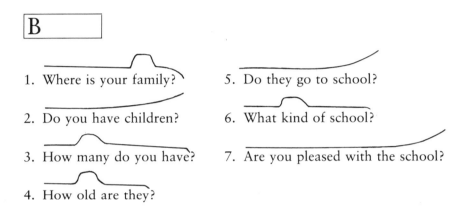

1. Where is your family?

2. Do you have children?

3. How many do you have?

4. How old are they?

5. Do they go to school?

6. What kind of school?

7. Are you pleased with the school?

Unit 16 • Thought groups

Listeners get the impression of smooth continuity when someone is talking. In fact, most speech is a sequence of brief stops and starts. These short sequences are based on the speaker's effort to organize thoughts around separate ideas. It helps the listener if the words around each idea are clearly grouped.

The demarcation of thought groups is part of clear speech because it is an aid to comprehension. Students need to be taught about thought group markers, because languages differ both in the way thought groups are marked and in the concept of what should be included in the group. For instance, although Indo-European languages use pauses to mark groups, many languages (Cantonese, Korean, and others) use clause-final particles (affixes) and therefore do not need to rely on intonation or timing to indicate group boundaries. Many languages, although they use pauses for this purpose, put boundaries in different places (French, Spanish, Japanese, Turkish, and others) (Ballmer 1980).

Because of these differences, students may not even notice pauses. In fact, they are nearly as important as the correct stress pattern of a word or correct emphasis on sentence focus. For instance, if there are no pauses in the customary places, the American listener may have difficulty understanding (mentally recording) a series of numbers, no matter how clearly each number is pronounced. In general, the "chunking" of language is a necessary mechanism to aid listener processing (Pribam 1980).

In English, thought group boundaries are marked by three basic signals:

1. Pause
2. Pitch drop
3. Lengthening of final syllable

The first two markers are discussed in the lecture in Unit 31. The third marker is probably too complicated for classroom use. At this point, students need only think about pausing to mark the end of a group.

You can use variations of the following techniques for additional practice:

1. Dictate phone numbers and addresses from a phone book. Put the answers on the board so that students can check their accuracy.
2. Have students dictate their own "number sets" to each other in pairs (phone numbers, addresses, passport numbers, etc.).

Give each student a card with a number set or sentence from the pairs in this lesson, to be read aloud to students writing at the board. This kind of dictation gives immediate visual feedback.

Practice filling pauses with common hesitation phrases: "ya know?," "well," "kay?," "I dunno," etc. This can be helpful in preparing students to hear actual colloquial speech where these phrases are common. It might be useful for students to know that these are just as empty of meaning as "mmm" and are used only as fillers or to encourage some response from the listener. There is also some social difference: "Ya know?" and "kay?" are generally used by younger speakers and may actually annoy some older people.

Unit 17 · Review

Basic emphasis pattern

Answers:

2. The <u>wife</u> is <u>meeting</u> with the <u>husband's</u> <u>assistant</u>.
3. A <u>detective</u> <u>has</u> a <u>tape</u> of their <u>conversation</u>.
4. He is <u>worried</u>.
5. Is the <u>husband</u> <u>planning</u> to <u>murder</u> them?

Focus

Answers:

2. The assistant is young.

3. Is the husband jealous?

4. They're planning to murder him.

5. The detective didn't really listen to it.

New focus

Answers:

POLICEMAN:	What are <u>you</u> doing here?
PRIVATE DETECTIVE:	I thought there was going to be a <u>murder</u>.
POLICEMAN:	Well, there <u>has</u> been. Did you <u>know</u> this man?
PRIVATE DETECTIVE:	I...mmm...I <u>thought</u> I did.
POLICEMAN:	<u>Tell</u> me what you know.
PRIVATE DETECTIVE:	I <u>thought</u> I knew a lot. But now I'm...<u>confused</u>.
POLICEMAN:	Mister, you're not making <u>any</u> <u>sense</u>. You'd better <u>come</u> with <u>me</u>.

Questions

Answers:

1. What's your name?

2. Where do you live?

34

3. Did you know the victim?

4. Why didn't you tell us?

5. Did you do it?

Thought groups

Answers:

1. Detective movies are popular   but so are comedies.
2. People can forget their troubles   and have a good time.
3. Acting is an old profession   because people love entertainment.
4. Some actors are in the newspapers all the time   and make a lot of
   money   but rock stars probably make more.

CLARITY OF SOUNDS

Unit 18 • Voicing

Many languages use voicing contrasts. Nonetheless, the contrast does not always transfer easily to perception of the new language, so it needs to be taught.

In a study of English as a Second Language pronunciation errors (Leahy 1980), it was found that the two principal types of errors were based on *voicing* (zoo/Sue: Units 18, 19) and *continuancy* (bus/but: Unit 20).

In voicing errors, the problem with stop sounds was found to be mainly in the final position (cap/cab) and was directly related to the length of the preceding vowel (Unit 19). The voicing errors with continuants occurred in all positions, not just finally (sink/zinc, ether/either, bus/buzz).

For practice in learning to hear voicing differences while saying them, just covering the ears will not be adequate. Tell students to press their hands *firmly* over their ears, to get the full effect of the contrast. The sound "z" should not be pronounced "zee" (like the alphabet name of the letter) but should be continued as "zzzz" (like a buzz). Similarly, the sound "s" should be continued as a hiss.

The voicing feature is a good way to help identify a difficult sound. Present an unfamiliar word like "grisly" (pronounced like "grizzly," as in grizzly bear). Ask the students if the "s" letter is voiced or unvoiced. Despite the spelling, the sound is voiced. You may want to use a word more likely to be useful, but this word was chosen because it is almost certain to be unknown. When the student has learned to recognize the difference between voiced and unvoiced sounds, this feature is an analytical tool for clearly hearing (and mentally recording) the pronunciation of a new word.

Write these sounds on the board: f   th   t   s   k   p
Ask for the voiced partner: (v   th   d   z   g   b)

It may help to present the contrasts in nonsense syllables (fay/vay, etc.). It is difficult to show the voicing difference for "th" without phonetic symbols. You could add a wavy line under "th" to show voicing:

unvoiced   *voiced*

thank   then

The main point of this exercise is for students to learn that two contrasting sounds can be made with the tongue in exactly the same position, but with a contrast in voicing.

A good way to practice these exercises (or any minimal pairs) is to give students scrambled lists of words to dictate to a partner.

Choose a statement and read it to the students. They must then give the correct response, depending on which word they hear. After a little of this practice, ask students to take turns testing the class this way.

Self-analysis

Answers:

    uv v   uv   v   v   uv
1. Sue/zoo, lacy/lazy, raising/racing

    v   uv   uv v   v   uv
2. vine/fine, fat/vat, leaving/leafing

    uv   v   uv   v   v   uv
3. thank/then, thin/then, either/ether

       uv   v   uv   v   v   uv   v   uv
4. We think that Sue is leaving sooner than we thought.

Unit 19 • Voicing and syllable length

Ask students to describe the pronunciation difference between the verb "use" and the noun "use." The answer has two parts: voicing of the final consonant and length of the vowel:

> <u>use</u> (verb): lengthened vowel, voiced consonant
> <u>use</u> (noun): shortened vowel, unvoiced consonant

The lengthened vowel helps the listener identify the final consonant:

      v   uv
> <u>lose</u> is longer than <u>loose</u>

A student might expect "loose" to take longer to say, because it looks longer in print. The extra length for "lose" may be especially puzzling to Japanese students, since "loose" may look like a double vowel. In Japanese, a double vowel is twice as long in speech as a single vowel. In English, a completely different rule is at work: the need to clearly identify the voicing of the following consonant.

Sometimes students get the mistaken notion that lengthening occurs because the voiced member of the pair is always second in the drill. So it is a good idea to do these lists a second time in reverse order.

The contrast between *Ms.* and *Miss* is a good opportunity to explain this new American title. *Ms.* is now generally used in business correspondence and is growing more common in spoken language. However, since it involves customs and philosophy, not everyone chooses to use the term. Some women prefer to be addressed by the new form, some by the old form:

> *Ms.   Miss   Mrs.* ("missuz")

Ask students to choose one of these alternative statements, testing the class or a partner to give the correct response.

Unit 20 • Stops and continuants

One graphic way to demonstrate the difference between stops and continuants is to say a continuant sound, "z," while walking back and forth in front of the class. You can continue such a sound as long as you still have air in your lungs. Now say a stop, "p." And stop. You simply cannot continue unless the "p" changes into a vowel or some other continuant.

Hand signals can aid correction during drills: The continuant can be represented by a pointed finger moving crosswise in front of your body (so as not to be pointing at anybody), and the stop can be represented by a nearly universal symbol, the palm of your hand facing the class.

C

Put the letters "p, t, k" on the board (pronounced "puh," "tuh," and "kuh"). Ask for their voiced versions as a review of previous units ("b, d, g"). Ask if these are stops or continuants.

Now the class has two ways to test a new or difficult-to-identify sound. Try testing several unfamiliar words, like "dedication." Just say the word, without writing it. Analyze the word syllable by syllable, checking the consonants with these questions:

1. Is it voiced?
2. Is it a stop?

It is easier to use a word without consonant clusters, since a word like "laundromat" is apt to confuse the lesson. The best words are ones the students may already have been puzzled by: words from their class or living situation. A good homework assignment is requiring them to notice such a word and to analyze it according to these two features.

Once students have a physical sense of the difference between stops and continuants, the contrast can be used to clarify a number of sound problems. The American "r" is difficult for Japanese, Spanish, Arabic, and other speakers, because the sound is made in their languages with a tap or trill of the tip of the tongue against the roof of the mouth. This is also common in some British dialects. It can cause confusion in an American context, however, because the native speaker automatically interprets it as a brief stop, much like the "t" in "city" or "beautiful."

Some students have a problem hearing the difference between "shoe" and "chew," and this hearing problem is often reflected in their speech. It is helpful to approach this as a contrast between a stop and a continuant. Phonetically speaking, "ch" and "dj" are affricates, not stops. But from a practical point of view, calling them stops helps the students analyze the difference. It is more exact to say that the sound *begins* with a stop. You can write the pair on the board and add some sort of "phonetic" spelling:

    shoe   (t)shoe

or write:

    share   chair   (t)share
    sheep   cheap   (t)sheep

The difference is the quick stop sound before the "ch" words.

If your students are confusing "yet" and "jet," use the same method, analyzing the first sounds as "yet," voiced continuant, and "jet," the quick stop sound "d" before the "zh" sound of measure.

Students from many language groups have trouble with the sound "v." If they are substituting something like "b," you can call their attention to the stop/continuant distinction. At this point you may want to skip ahead to the lesson on this sound problem, if it is a major difficulty for most of your students.

Some students substitute "tank" for "thank." This might be helped by pointing out the difference between the stop and continuant features of these sounds. Usually substitutions are systematic and based on a feature like voicing and continuancy, so that awareness of these features can help clarify a number of different sound difficulties.

Answer: Group 1 ends with a continuant sound.

Unit 21 • Puff of air (aspiration)

A

The "puff of air" (aspiration) is probably stronger at the beginning of a word than in the middle, but the simple distinction of with/without the puff is difficult enough for most students to think about.

This unit is especially helpful for Spanish and Arabic speakers, or for anyone from a language group that has difficulty distinguishing the stop sounds according to their voicing. For many students it is an easier way of differentiating the stops, rather than trying to clarify the voicing differences (pole/bowl). It is easier to practice, and it may be easier to hear. A Spanish speaker named Perez, for instance, probably has difficulty getting an American to understand the spelling of the name. Even if the "p" stop is said without voicing, unless the American hears aspiration, the sound is likely to be judged a "b." Similarly, the common Arabic pronunciation of a popular cola drink, "Bebsi," can be clarified greatly by the addition of aspiration to the initial stop.

Unit 22 • Linking words

Linking is a major source of comprehension difficulty for English learners, so it is worth practicing it in as many ways as possible.

A

In the phrase, "the end," the vowel in "the" is not reduced, because it comes before another vowel. Other examples you could practice this with include:

> the apple   the answer   the order   the animals

B

Stop-to-stop: It may help your Japanese students to understand the effect of two of the same stops said together if you ask them how they say a word like "Sapporo." The impression of a slight hesitation before completing the stop is similar to the English "stop pushing."

E

Songs can be used to practice the English way of moving a consonant to the next syllable. The old popular song "Mairzy Doats" was written based on this principle ("Mares eat oats").

If you think about your own favorite songs this way, you will probably find one that can be used to demonstrate this characteristic of English.

Unit 23 • Review

Reduction and linking

Dictation:

1. Is she going to tell (h)im the news?
2. Is (h)e busy this afternoon?
3. Give (h)er the old ones first.
4. Send (h)im all of our records.
5. You ought to tell me.

LISTENING

Unit 24 • Listening accuracy

Play the Cassette or read the dictation aloud, and ask students only to follow the meaning, not to write. Then dictate the script (or play the Cassette), pausing between phrases, while the students write. After the dictation, read the whole script through again. These sentences are very long, so it is hard for the listener to keep track of the structure. The third reading may help them notice errors caused by misunderstanding the development of thought.

After the dictation, ask students to compare their work with the script, and mark errors, especially checking for the following: missing reduced words (was, should) and prepositions (of, in). The main point of this exercise is to alert your students to the fact that they may not be hearing words that are usually reduced. If the words are missing from a student's dictation, they are probably missing from the student's speech and writing as well.

This is also a good time to demonstrate the need for careful proofreading. Collect the papers and mark the remaining errors. If their proofreading has been inadequate, they need to know it now. This second check alerts students to the need for an improved proofreading technique. You might suggest that they proofread by reading aloud or, if the work is really important (a university essay, for instance), they should get a friend to read it aloud while they proofread.

Unit 25 • Hearing numbers

Many people are made uneasy by "foreign food," but chocolate chip cookies meet with little resistance, so they make good ambassadors of good will for American culture. This lesson can be made more real by bringing measuring utensils to class and discussing metric versus American measures. With some luck, you might be able to talk one or more students into making a batch of cookies for the class!

Read the recipe that appears on page 68 of the Student's Book, while students fill in the numbers they hear. Answers:

Ingredients

½ cup or _113_ grams white sugar
½ cup or _113_ grams brown sugar
⅔ cup or _168_ grams butter
1 egg
_1_ teaspoon or _5_ ml vanilla
1½ cups or _215_ grams flour

½ teaspoon or _2.5_ grams salt
½ teaspoon or _2.5_ grams baking soda
¾ cup or _85_ grams nuts
_6_ ounces or _170_ grams chocolate chips

Method

Heat the oven to _375_ °
Fahrenheit or _190_ ° Celsius.
Mix sugars, butter, egg, and
vanilla thoroughly. Stir in
remaining ingredients.
Drop dough by rounded
teaspoonfuls about _2_
inches or _5_ centimeters
apart on ungreased cookie
sheet. Bake _8_ to _10_ minutes
until light brown.
Cool slightly before removing
from cookie sheet. This recipe
makes about _3½_ dozen cookies,
which is _42_ individual cookies.

Cookies are a big business in the U.S. One shop in Boston sells _30,000_ warm cookies every day, mostly chocolate chip. On the West Coast, a _45_-year-old American, Wally Amos, has made his fortune from chocolate chip cookies.

When Amos was _13_ years old, he went to live with his Aunt Delia, who made cookies for him, from a recipe created in _1929_. Amos joined the Air Force in _1953_, and his aunt sent him cookies so he wouldn't be homesick. For Amos, as for most Americans, cookies represent love and home.

After the Air Force, Amos worked for other people for _14_ years. In _1975_, he decided he could make more money if he had his own business. He talked some friends into investing _$24,500_ in a cookie business. He worked _18_ hours a day, baking cookies and thinking of clever ways to promote them. For instance, he traded _$750_ worth of cookies for advertising time on a local radio station. In _1976_, he began selling cookies in _15_ department stores on the East Coast. That year the cookie corporation took in _$300,000_. By _1982_ the company made _$7,000,000_. Amos now has _150_ employees, and they produce more than _7,000_ pounds of cookies a day.

Unit 26 • Getting essential information

This is an actual map of the O'Hare International Airport in Chicago. Airport arrangements vary in different U.S. cities, but the vocabulary is useful for all.

Do you have a pencil and something to write on? O.K. Well, the first thing is that your plane will arrive at Gate E4. When you come out of the gate, turn to the right. Look for the signs that say Terminal and Baggage Claim. If you follow those signs, you'll get to terminal 2. Then you have to look for signs saying Delta Airlines. Follow them until you get to the right terminal for Delta. Don't stop to buy a newspaper or anything because you won't have time. When you get to the Delta terminal area, go through the security check. After the security check, keep going toward the Delta gates. You'll see TV screens for information up on the walls. Look for one that says Delta.

The TV screens show all the arrivals and departures, but you just look under departures for your Atlanta flight. Remember that your flight number is 236, and it's supposed to leave for Atlanta at 5:13. If you look to the right of the flight number, you'll see the gate number. Then you better get there fast.

B

1. E4
2. right
3. Terminal and Baggage Claim
4. 2
5. Delta Airlines
6. Delta terminal area
7. under departures
8. 236
9. 5:13
10. to the right of the flight number

C

The line should be drawn from E4 to H3.

Unit 27 • Listening comprehension (taking notes)

Read the paragraph aloud, or play the Cassette, while students read it silently. Have the class, with books closed, listen as you read again (or rewind the Cassette and play the lecture again). Students then write what they remember. Then you, or a student acting as clerk for the class, can put notes on the board, as agreed to by class discussion. Or several students can put their different versions on the board.

The main object of this unit is to practice cutting down on superfluous words. It is also a good time to introduce the subject of outlining.

The distinction between main points and supporting ideas is extremely difficult for some students. This may be because of cultural differences. Some societies place a very high value on analytical, sequential presentations of ideas. Other societies place more value on formulaic speech, fixed expressions that are combined to emphasize shared feeling. This can produce a very different sense of what is important about a narrative (Tannen 1981).

Especially when you are dealing with written text, the question of which words are more important simply may not make sense. As one writer commented:

> In Islamic countries, the Koran is in back of the reader's mind when dealing with a text. Hence what is written is necessarily associated with absolute truth...the reader regards the text as a fixed unit in which everything is of equal importance. Text is, so to speak, a plateau rather than a hierarchical structure of statements. [Osterloh 1980, p. 65]

Whatever the reasons may be for students' difficulty in distinguishing main points from lesser ideas, they need to gain this skill in order to take effective lecture notes. One way you can help students begin to think about identifying major ideas is to ask questions like these, based on the paragraph in this unit:

1. Why is skill at note taking important? (must use notes to study for exam)
2. Why is it wrong to try to write every word? (not enough time)
3. What words are most important? (new information/focus words)
4. How can you recognize these words? (intonation/highlighting)

Unit 28 • *Listening comprehension: Age and Language Learning*

B

Answers:

1. d   2. c   3. d

The subject matter of this exercise was chosen for a pep-talk purpose. Most adult language learners believe that pronunciation is a more or less hopeless task at their age. This sense of discouragement keeps some students from making any real effort to improve. This produces a self-fulfilling prophecy; a student who makes no effort does not improve. For this reason, it is important to encourage students to believe that they are personally capable of considerable improvement.

This is a TOEFL-length lecture, but the format is different, since the students are reading the script. The next unit is closer to actual TOEFL conditions.

Unit 29 • Listening comprehension: Guides to Universities

These questions are recorded on the Cassette. After each question, stop the tape for a few seconds to give the students time to select the correct answer in the Student's Book. If you read the questions aloud, pause for a few seconds between questions.

Questions:	*Answers*:
1. What was the main topic of this talk?	b
2. What can you find in a general guide to universities?	c
3. According to the speaker, what is one reason you should write for a catalogue?	c
4. What is tuition?	d
5. What does the word "housing" mean?	c

Unit 30 • Lecture: Pronunciation Achievement Factors

One very simple approach to this lecture is to have students take turns reading it aloud. A problem with this is that some people have trouble understanding the meaning of something they are reading aloud. On the other hand, reading aloud is an excellent way to practice phrasing (thought grouping) stress patterns and highlighting the focus words.

A more advanced approach (closer to university work) is to play the Cassette or read the lecture to the students while they take notes. Halfway through the lecture, ask the class to dictate the basic points for you to write on the board. Did they get a clear idea of the subject? Did they recognize the aim of the research? (What was the researcher trying to test? How was the research carried out? How were the variables tested? How many variables were tested?)

After the full lecture, ask students to list the results and give a summary conclusion, perhaps something like "Two of the most important variables are under the student's control."

One way to help sharpen note-taking skills is the "reverse construction" exercise. Ask students to compare their notes with partners, as a preparation for reconstructing the lecture. One team could be responsible for the first third of the lecture, another for the second third, and so on.

Going from the full lecture to an outline and then back to a full lecture is a very high-level, demanding intellectual task. Students may object that this is "teacher's work," because they often assume that their sole responsibility is to absorb facts. You can remind them that your aim is to help them learn to take effective notes. The quality of their understanding of the main structure of a lecture will be a decisive part of their academic success. The reverse construction process is another way to practice getting the main points. If they can re-create a rough facsimile of the lecture, based on their notes, they will be well prepared for any examination.

An alternative way to use these lectures is to have a student clerk taking notes at the board while you lecture. One-third of the way through, stop and ask the class to compare their own notes with those on the board. Are all essential ideas present? Could some words be omitted? Continue the lecture in the same way.

Students will develop their own method of taking notes and their own judgment of what material they must record. So the class discussion of notes should not have a correct/incorrect emphasis. The purpose is to stimulate individual analytical thinking and active choice.

Unit 31 • Lecture: Thought Group Markers

Play the Cassette or read the lecture while the students take notes. Another approach is to give the lecture from your own outline, rather than reading.

In order to help students follow this lecture, and also to demonstrate a helpful technique for oral reports, be careful to write the examples on the board. Write O'Malley's name when it is first mentioned, as a note-taking aid. The algebraic formulas should be written on the board when first mentioned. Afterward they can be pointed to, as you read them aloud, demonstrating the particular marker you are describing (pauses or pitch changes). It is a good idea to exaggerate the marker when you say the examples aloud.

This is a good time to go over the exercises in Unit 16 (Thought Groups) to reinforce the work from that unit. The purpose of this lecture (aside from practicing note taking) is to help students recognize the pitch-fall marker for the end of the group, as well as to give further attention to the basic concept of thought groups. Students can benefit by being reminded that language should be processed in thought groups, not one word at a time.

Unit 32 • Lecture: Techniques for Oral Presentation

Whatever method you use for summarizing the notes on this lecture (group dictation to another student at the board, pair-work summaries, etc.), the class should end up with a list of rules for good oral reports. This list can then be incorporated into a "judging sheet," which can be used for evaluating fellow students' presentations (Unit 34).

After this unit, you can assign a day for each student's report or pass around a sign-up sheet for them to choose a day. The talk should be limited to 5–10 minutes, depending on the level of the students. They should be warned that they will be judged partly on their observance of these techniques, as well as the thoroughness of preparation. Many students will not have previously realized that they have an obligation to make their talks comprehensible, as well as thorough.

Since this oral report should be similar to a university or business presentation, the students will need time to prepare properly. You may want to direct them to conduct some library research.

During the week or more in which you allow them this preparation time (depending on the organization of your course), the class hours can be spent with students' own dictation. Ask them to bring a long sentence (or two short sentences) from a book or article in a field that interests them (see Unit 33).

CLEAR SPEECH

Unit 33 • Student's own dictation

If the relationship between speaker and listener is like an electrical circuit, then this exercise can be thought of as a "circuit breakdown analysis." It is a time-consuming activity, but it can be extraordinarily rewarding.

The exercise works this way: Students are asked to bring one or two long sentences from their own field. You may not be able to complete more than a few dictations at each class session, but students can save their sentences until you get to them. Tell the class that they are going to dictate these sentences, but this is not going to be a listening test for the class. Students will be writing what they hear dictated in order to help the speaker analyze his or her own speech weaknesses. This can be useful for everybody, since most errors are typical, and students should be using the exercise to learn to avoid making the same mistakes. Group help for a fellow student can build rapport in a class, if it is not allowed to become group criticism.

Before starting the dictation, the speaker should write any unusual terms (especially technical jargon) on the board. Then the sentences should be read aloud so that the class can hear the whole piece. If possible, this should be recorded. Now the speaker should dictate the sentences. Students should write what they hear, leaving blank spaces for words they cannot catch. Finally, the speaker should read the sentences again so that students can check their work.

Ask the speaker and two or three students to write their versions on the board. The listeners' versions can now be compared with the original.

Caution 1: This exercise is likely to be more successful in a mixed-language class. If the students all speak the same language, they understand each other's English, because their errors are all the same.

Caution 2: Students sometimes express doubts about the value of taking dictation from a non-native speaker. The teacher can reassure the class that the exercise is valuable for both speaker and class, because it is often possible to distinguish between listener errors and speaker errors.

Analysis procedure

Take dictation yourself, while the students are writing. Note all the errors you can. In particular, errors in emphasis and thought grouping are not likely to be noticed by the class, so you will need to have a record of them.

Circle the content words. If a content word is missing (or there is a serious sound error in it), the confusion is apt to extend for several words following, since the listener is still trying to identify the first word. Also, the content word error may cause a mistaken idea later, as the listener tries to make sense of the sentence. For instance, if a noun is thought to be a verb (or vice versa), there is bound to be confusion later.

Syllables are frequently dropped, either in unstressed prefixes or (more commonly) in final syllables. Final "s" is the most common error.

Individual sound errors often fall into the categories of the stop/continuant contrast or the voiced/unvoiced contrast. This provides you with the opportunity for reviewing these differences.

It is not always easy to tell if the error was a speaking mistake or a listening mistake, but some patterns are easily recognizable. For instance, if a speaker pronounced "of" as "off," it is likely that some of the students will write it that way. This is a speaker error, not a listener error. On the other hand, if you know that the speaker said "present" and several students wrote "pleasant," you can point it out as a listener error.

If you are a native speaker of English and an experienced teacher of the language, your ear will have a tendency to correct errors automatically, so that you may not notice them. However, even if you did not note the error yourself, you can probably assume that the speaker made a mistake if several class members (from different language groups) wrote the same thing.

If there was an unfamiliar idiom or word, students are apt to miss it and maybe also get confused for several words following. This is a good time to point out the importance of pronouncing an unusual term with special care.

Analysis of these dictations can provide a practical summary of everything you have taught the students in this course. After this analysis, and some class practice of the sentence, the student can record the dictation again, for comparison with the first version.

Unit 34 • Student's oral report

Be strict about the time allowance. It promotes more careful planning if the speaker knows the time is limited.

Most teachers realize that language practice is more effective if there is a genuine communicative intent, if the speaker is telling the listeners something they did not already know. This lesson should be a natural way to put that principle into action. Unfortunately, traditionally trained students quite frequently see this sort of exercise as simply another way for the speaker to practice correct English, while the class, politely deaf, thinks about other things. Students may need help recognizing that they have a responsibility beyond correctness. As speakers, they have a responsibility to make their report easily understandable; as listeners, they have a responsibility to make an effort to understand.

One way to overcome a reluctance to accept mutual responsibility is to use a traditional tool, testing. Ask each speaker to prepare three questions for a quiz on the talk. The class should take notes during the talk to prepare for the quiz.

The questions can be read aloud after the talk. If most of the class can answer the questions, then the point was clearly conveyed. On the other hand, if the class as a whole cannot answer (i.e., give the answer the speaker considers correct), you can ask, "How can this talk be improved so that you would have been able to answer that question?" The resulting discussion can be a review of the suggestions in Unit 32 (Techniques for Oral Presentations). The speaker can help the audience remember a main point by paraphrasing it at least once. Another helpful suggestion is to re-state the idea in the conclusion of the talk. A surprising number of students are unaware of the effectiveness of a concluding summary.

A useful way to look at the "failed" question is that the point of the question may not have been worth much attention. Students often write questions on details, simply because they are easy to write or because the student thinks the purpose of a quiz question is to be difficult. It is important for the class to realize that the main function of this post-talk quiz is to test the true effectiveness of the talk. Also, the students should begin to see that the formulation of the questions is a way to determine which main thoughts they really want their talk to convey. Not only does this encourage them to limit the amount of information in their reports, but it gives them the beginning of a strong structure, or outline. Clear structure is the necessary basis for a clear talk.

A final exercise for each oral report could be small group preparations of a summary sentence, based on the students' notes. Summarization is a high-level intellectual exercise; it requires deep attention and understanding of the substance of the report. The value of the exercise is that it causes students to focus on the communication of ideas rather than on narrow correctness of language.

Unit 35 • Problem sound contrasts: consonants

Some students are helped by a picture of the mouth making a sound, but many are confused when they first see such a picture. You can help them get oriented if, instead of presenting them with a complete drawing, you draw it while they watch. It does not matter how anatomically accurate the drawing is if you describe it while you draw. Mention each part (eye, nose, lip) as the chalk line moves, so they understand clearly which direction the profile is turned.

As you draw the upper lip, ask students to touch their own lip with the tip of their tongue. Then have them follow the chalk line around the lip, over the front teeth, over the tooth ridge bump, up the roof of the mouth, and back as far as they can reach. Since this activity is invisible, it is private, so you will have a high level of participation. It draws the students' attention to the parts you are mentioning in the most immediate way possible and truly orients them to your profile drawing. No matter how unrealistic the sketch is, the students are getting a direct kinesthetic relationship to the drawing. This tongue-tip experience prepares them for later directions, such as, "Place the tip of your tongue on the tooth ridge." It makes them realize that the sharp V-shape behind the lip really does represent their front teeth. This is not easily accepted usually, since the V-shape does not fit the mental image most of us have of our front teeth, which, after all, are never seen from the side.

The V-shape of the front teeth can be a handy memory device for practicing the "v" sound. The critical feature of a "v" is that the upper teeth must remain in contact with the lower lip. When students see the letter "v" in print, remind them to think of the picture of the upper front teeth, which are in a V-shape. Since many students have been reading English for some time and have been reacting to the "v" letter with a wrong mental image of the sound that is appropriate, this teeth image may help dislodge the wrong pattern.

Another habitually wrong image can occur with the letters "r" and "l" when seen in print. Suggest to the students that they think of the letter "r" as short and bunched up, like the tongue drawn back for the "r" sound. The "l" sound is made with a long tongue, reaching to touch the tooth ridge, and shaped rather like the letter "l" in print.

The "r" sound can be practiced with an ice cream stick or a roll of aluminum foil sideways in the mouth. This discourages touching the tip of the tongue to the roof of the mouth.

Tongue-between-the-teeth sounds (interdental: "th") are rare in other languages. They may be embarrassing for some students to practice because of the feeling that it is impolite (even disgusting) to show one's tongue. Practice with a small mirror can be helpful, both because it shows the student's tongue tip and because it prevents the mouth from being seen by others. An even more private way to practice is with a plastic deflector, which covers the mouth and conveys sound directly to the student's ears. These deflectors, which can be found in elementary school developmental skills catalogues, greatly increase students' ability to monitor their own production. Some language lab facilities can also give this direct hearing experience, as the voice goes directly into the person's ears rather than being dispersed in the air.

In general, it is important to be sensitive to students' embarrassment, because it has such a constraining effect. Pronunciation seems much more affected by strain than other kinds of language skills. Therefore, choral practice may be more effective, even though it makes teacher monitoring more difficult.

Unit 36 • Vowels

There is some research evidence to suggest that vowels, unlike consonants, are best learned initially through listening perception drills rather than speaking practice (Fucci et al. 1977). That is why most of the vowel exercises here concentrate mainly on auditory perception practice.

Since vowels improve only very gradually, the most practical approach is to have modest expectations. If you hope for good English vowels by the end of the course, the result is apt to be discouraging. Perhaps the most we can do (and it is really quite a lot) is to teach students how to listen for these vowels, sorting them into English categories. If the students have developed a belief that pronunciation is important (Unit 30) and possible (Unit 28), then listening to spoken English will gradually shape their vowels closer to the English target sounds.

For answers, see Student's Book, pp. 90, 91.

Quiz 1
(Unit 1 · Syllables)

A. Listen to the following words read twice. Mark the number of syllables for each word.

Example: bus_1_   busses_2_   original_4_

1. ____
2. ____
3. ____
4. ____
5. ____

B. Listen to the following sentences. You will hear one from each pair. One is correct and one is not complete. If you hear the correct sentence, write "Right." If you hear the incomplete sentence, write "Wrong."

1a. Yesterday she rented a bike.

 b. Yesterday she rent a bike.   _____

2a. He wishes you would come.

 b. He wish you would come.   _____

3a. We need a radio.

 b. We need radio.   _____

4a. The shoes are under the table.

 b. The shoes are under table.   _____

5a. The bus is here.

 b. The bus here.   _____

(Count 10 points for each correct answer.)

Quiz 2
(Unit 2 • Pitch)

Name_____

Date_____

    A. Listen to the following names of states in the United States. Draw a pitch pattern for each name.

1. Ohio

2. California

3. Florida

4. Alabama

5. Nevada

    B. Listen to the following sentences. Draw a pitch line for each sentence:

1. I can't tell you.

2. You lost your pen?

3. What did they say?

4. How long have you been here?

5. How long have they been here?

(Count 10 points for each correct answer. If the pitch rise is not on the correct syllable, count zero. The exact placement is important.)

Quiz 3
(Unit 3 • Length)

A. Listen to the following words. Underline the word with the longer vowel.

Example: <u>may</u> mate

1. why   white
2. seat   see
3. cute   cue
4. lie   light
5. loose   lose

6. use (verb)   use (noun)
7. plays   place
8. low   load
9. sigh   sight
10. be   beat

B. Listen to the following words. Did you hear pattern A or pattern B? Write the letter after the word.

A: s͞ofa   B: allo͞w

1. summer   —
2. winter   —
3. lengthen   —
4. widen   —
5. reverse   —

6. orange   —
7. purple   —
8. about   —
9. above   —
10. under   —

(Count 5 points for each correct answer.)

Quiz 4
(Unit 4 • Clarity)

A. Listen to these words. Underline the full vowels (one in each word).

1. banana
2. apply
3. formal
4. atom
5. given

6. criminal
7. atomic
8. allowance
9. medical
10. payment

B. Listen to the following sentences using the singular and plural form of the word "woman." Write the word that is missing:

1. Say the word _____ now.

2. The word you want is _____.

3. How do you spell _____?

4. _____ is a confusing word.

5. We can practice reduced vowels with the word _____.

(Count 5 points for each correct answer in section A. Count 10 points for each correct answer in section B.)

Quiz 5
(Unit 6 • Stress patterns)

A. Listen and then underline the word that you hear.

1. thirteen   thirty
2. fifteen   fifty
3. fourteen   forty
4. nineteen   ninety
5. eighteen   eighty

B. Listen to two words. Are the stress patterns of the words the same or different? Write "S" for same and "D" for different:

Example: under   over   <u>S</u>

1. Alaska   Florida   —
2. register   economy   —
3. agriculture   technology   —
4. engineering   registration   —
5. permission   imagine   —

(Count 10 points for each correct answer.)

Quiz 6
(Unit 12 • Sentence focus)

Read this dialogue. Underline one focus word for each remark.

A: What do you do for exercise?

B: Well, nothing, I guess.

A: You should, you know.

B: Yes, but I don't like it.

A: Why not?

B: Because it's boring.

A: Not if you exercise in a sport.

B: What kind of sport?

A: Well, tennis, for example.

B: Tennis is too much work.

(Count 10 points for each correct focus.)

Name_____

Date_____

Quiz 7
(Unit 19 • Voicing and syllable length)

Listen to the following words. Is the underlined consonant voiced or unvoiced? Write "V" or "UV" after each word.

1. lea<u>v</u>e ____
2. pri<u>c</u>e ____
3. <u>th</u>ought ____
4. bu<u>zz</u>er ____
5. o<u>th</u>er ____
6. ra<u>c</u>ing ____
7. bro<u>th</u>er ____
8. abo<u>v</u>e ____
9. arri<u>v</u>e ____
10. kni<u>f</u>e ____

11. brea<u>the</u> ____
12. flie<u>s</u> ____
13. lo<u>s</u>e ____
14. loo<u>s</u>e ____
15. excu<u>s</u>e ____ (noun)
16. ba<u>ck</u> ____
17. brea<u>k</u> ____
18. ru<u>g</u> ____
19. re<u>d</u> ____
20. be<u>d</u> ____

(Count 5 points for each correct answer.)

Name_____

Date_____

Quiz 8
(Unit 20 • Stops and continuants)

Listen to the following sentences. You will hear one from each pair. Put an "X" next to the one you hear.

1a. What are you watching? ___

  b. What are you washing? ___

2a. Do you like soup? ___

  b. Do you like Sue? ___

3a. What does "fair" mean? ___

  b. What does "pair" mean? ___

4a. Does he have a vote? ___

  b. Does he have a boat? ___

5a. Did you say "thought"? ___

  b. Did you say "taught"? ___

6a. What's the date? ___

  b. What's the rate? ___

7a. Do you have a chair? ___

  b. Do you have a share? ___

8a. That's a light. ___

  b. That's a lie. ___

9a. What's a ram? ___

  b. What's a dam? ___

10a. Did you say "very"? ___

  b. Did you say "berry"? ___

(Count 10 points for each correct answer.)

Answers to quizzes

Quiz 1 (page 54)

A. 1. hotel (2)
   2. clothing (2)
   3. suitcases (3)
   4. baggage (2)
   5. university (5)

B. 1. Yesterday she rent a bike.   Wrong
   2. He wishes you would come.   Right
   3. We need a radio.   Right
   4. The shoes are under table.   Wrong
   5. The bus here.   Wrong

Quiz 2 (page 55)

A. 1. Ohio   3. Florida   5. Nevada

   2. California   4. Alabama

B. 1. I can't tell you.   4. How long have you been here?

   2. You lost your pen?   5. How long have they been here?

   3. What did they say?

Quiz 3 (page 56)

A. 1. why white   6. use (verb) use (noun)
   2. seat see   7. plays place
   3. cute cue   8. low load
   4. lie light   9. sigh sight
   5. loose lose   10. be beat

B. 1. summer   A   6. orange   A
   2. winter   A   7. purple   A
   3. lengthen   A   8. about   B
   4. widen   A   9. above   B
   5. reverse   B   10. under   A

Quiz 4 (page 57)

A. 1. banana   6. criminal
    2. apply   7. atomic
    3. formal   8. allowance
    4. atom   9. medical
    5. given   10. payment

B. 1. Say the word woman now.
    2. The word you want is women.
    3. How do you spell women?
    4. Woman is a confusing word.
    5. We can practice reduced vowels with the word women.

Quiz 5 (page 58)

A. 1. thirteen   thirty
    2. fifteen   fifty
    3. fourteen   forty
    4. nineteen   ninety
    5. eighteen   eighty

B. 1. Alaska   Florida   D
    2. register   economy   D
    3. agriculture   technology   D
    4. engineering   registration   S
    5. permission   imagine   S

Quiz 6 (page 59)

A: What do you do for exercise?
B: Well, nothing, I guess.
A: You should, you know.
B: Yes, but I don't like it.
A: Why not?
B: Because it's boring.
A: Not if you exercise in a sport.
B: What kind of sport?
A: Well, tennis, for example.
B: Tennis is too much work.

Quiz 7 (page 60)

1. leave   V   11. breathe   V
2. price   UV   12. flies   V
3. thought   UV   13. lose   V
4. buzzer   V   14. loose   UV

5. other	V	15. excuse	UV (noun)
6. racing	UV	16. back	UV
7. brother	V	17. break	UV
8. above	V	18. rug	V
9. arrive	V	19. red	V
10. knife	UV	20. bed	V

Quiz 8 (page 61)

1a.	What are you watching?	—
b.	What are you washing?	X
2a.	Do you like soup?	—
b.	Do you like Sue?	X
3a.	What does "fair" mean?	X
b.	What does "pair" mean?	—
4a.	Does he have a vote?	X
b.	Does he have a boat?	—
5a.	Did you say "thought"?	X
b.	Did you say "taught"?	—
6a.	What's the date?	—
b.	What's the rate?	X
7a.	Do you have a chair?	X
b.	Do you have a share?	—
8a.	That's a light.	X
b.	That's a lie.	—
9a.	What's a ram?	—
b.	What's a dam?	X
10a.	Did you say "very"?	X
b.	Did you say "berry"?	—

Problem sound contrasts listed by languages

pin/bin

Arabic
Chinese
Korean
Spanish
Thai (final)
Turkish
Vietnamese

pan/fan

Arabic
Hindi
Indonesian
Korean
Tagalog
Telugu
Thai (final)
Turkish
Vietnamese

van/ban

Arabic
Farsi
Japanese
Indonesian
Korean
Spanish
Tagalog

chin/shin

Arabic
Farsi
Korean
Portuguese
Spanish
Tagalog
Tamil
Thai
Vietnamese

thin/tin

Arabic (Libyan)
Farsi
Indonesian
Japanese
Korean
Portuguese
Russian
Spanish
Tagalog
Tamil
Telugu
Thai
Turkish
Vietnamese

thin/sin

Arabic
Chinese
Farsi
French
Indonesian
Japanese
Korean
Russian
Spanish
Tagalog
Tamil
Vietnamese

rack/lack

Chinese
Japanese
Korean
Thai (initial)
Vietnamese

Bibliography

Allen, Virginia F. (1971). Teaching intonation, from theory to practice. *TESOL Quarterly* 4 (March): 73–81.

Ballmer, Thomas T. (1980). The role of pauses and suprasegmentals in a grammar. In *Temporal Variables in Speech*, H. Dechert and M. Raupach (eds.), pp. 211–220. Mouton, The Hague.

Bogen, Joseph E. (1975). Some educational aspects of hemispheric specialization. *UCLA Educator* 17: 24–32.

Bolinger, Dwight L. (1958). Intonation and grammar. *Language Learning* 8: 31–117.

Bolinger, Dwight L. (1961). *Forms of English*. Harvard University Press, Cambridge, Mass.

Bolinger, Dwight L. (1981). *Two Kinds of Vowels, Two Kinds of Rhythm*. University of Indiana Linguistics Club, Bloomington.

Bowen, J. Donald (1972). Contextualizing pronunciation practice in the ESL classroom. *TESOL Quarterly* 6 (March): 83–94.

Bowen, J. Donald (1975). *Patterns of English Pronunciation*. Newbury House, Rowley, Mass.

Brazil, David; Coulthard, Malcolm; and Johns, Catherine (1980). *Discourse Intonation and Language Teaching*. Longman, London.

Brown, Gillian (1977). *Listening to Spoken English*. Longman, London.

Brown, Gillian (1978). Understanding spoken language. *TESOL Quarterly* 12 (Sept.): 271–284.

Chafe, Wallace L. (1970). *Meaning and the Structure of Language*. University of Chicago Press.

Crowell, Thomas L. Jr. (1961). *Modern Spoken English*. McGraw-Hill, New York.

Daneš, Frantisek (1960). Sentence intonation from a functional point of view. *Word* 16: 34–54.

de Bot, Kees, and Mailfert, Kate (1982). The teaching of intonation: fundamental research and classroom applications. *TESOL Quarterly* 16(1): 71–77.

Fry, Dennis (1955). Duration and intensity as physical correlates of linguistic stress. *Journal of the Acoustical Society of America* 27: 765–768.

Fucci, D.; Crary, M.; Warren, J.; and Bond, Z. (1977). Interaction between auditory and oral sensory feedback in speech regulation. *Perceptual and Motor Skills* 45: 123–129.

Gilbert, Judy B. (1978). Gadgets: nonverbal tools for teaching pronunciation. *CATESOL Occasional Papers* 4: 68–78.

Gilbert, Judy B. (1980). Prosodic development: some pilot studies. In *Research in Second Language Acquisition*, S. Krashen and R. Scarcella (eds.), pp. 110–117. Newbury House, Rowley, Mass.

Gilbert, Judy B. (1982). Pronunciation, an aid to listening comprehension. *CATESOL Occasional Papers* 8:62–71.

Gilbert, Judy B. (1983). Pronunciation and listening comprehension. *Cross Currents*, Vol. X, No. 1 (Spring): 53–61.

Graham, Carolyn (1978). *Jazz Chants*. Oxford University Press, New York.

Grosjean, François (1980). Comparative studies of temporal variables in spoken and sign languages. In *Temporal Variables in Speech*, H. Dechert and M. Raupach (eds.), pp. 307–312. Mouton, The Hague.

Gumperz, John, and Kaltman, Hannah (1980). Prosody, linguistic diffusion and conversational inference. *Berkeley Linguistic Society* 6: 44–65.

Hatch, Evelyn (1977). Optimal age or optimal learners? *Workpapers in Teaching English as a Second Language* X: 45–56. University of California, Los Angeles.

Huggins, A. W. F. (1979). Some effects on intelligibility of inappropriate temporal relations within speech units. *Proceedings of the Ninth International Congress of Phonetic Sciences*, Vol. 12. University of Copenhagen, Institute of Phonetics.

Krashen, Stephen; Long, Michael; and Scarcella, Robin (1979). Age, rate, and eventual attainment in second language acquisition. *TESOL Quarterly* 13: 573–582.

Leahy, R. (1980). A practical approach for teaching ESL pronunciation based on distinctive feature analysis. *TESOL Quarterly* 14: 209–306.

Lehiste, Ilse (1977). Isochrony reconsidered. *Journal of Phonetics*, 5: 253–263.

Meyer, George A. (1968). *Speaking Fluent American English*. The National Press, Palo Alto.

Morley, Joan (1979). *Improving Spoken English*. University of Michigan Press, Ann Arbor.

Nash, Rose (1971). Phonemic and prosodic interference and their effects on intelligibility. *Proceedings of the Seventh International Congress of Phonetic Sciences*: 138–139.

Nilsen, D., and Nilsen, A. (1971). *Pronunciation Contrasts in English*. Regents Publishing Co., New York.

Ohala, John, and Gilbert, Judy B. (1981). Listener's ability to identify languages by their prosody. *Studia Phonetica* 18: 123–132.

Osterloh, K-H. (1980). Intercultural differences and communicative approaches to foreign language teaching in the Third World. *Studies in Second Language Acquisition* 3: 64–70. Indiana University Press, Bloomington.

Prator, Clifford, and Robinett, Betty (1972). *Manual of American English Pronunciation*, 3rd ed. Holt, Rinehart and Winston, New York.

Pribam, Karl (1980). The place of pragmatics in the syntactic and semantic organization of language. In *Temporal Variables in Speech*, H. Dechert and M. Raupach (eds.), pp. 13–20. Mouton, The Hague.

Tannen, Deborah (1981). Implications of the oral/literate continuum for cross-cultural communication. In *Georgetown University Round Table on Languages and Linguistics 1980: Current Issues in Bilingualism*, J. Alatis (ed.), pp. 327–345. Georgetown University Press, Washington, D.C.

Wong, Rita (1987). *Teaching Pronunciation: Focus on English Rhythm and Intonation*. Copublished by the Center for Applied Linguistics and Prentice-Hall, Englewood Cliffs, N.J.